New Routes to English

Beginning Skills/One

STUDENT BOOK

Senior Author
Gloria Paulik Sampson

ASSOCIATE PROFESSOR OF EDUCATION
SIMON FRASER UNIVERSITY, BRITISH COLUMBIA

Collier Macmillan Canada, Ltd.

STAFF

NEW ROUTES TO ENGLISH

PROJECT EDITOR: Judith Reeves-Stevens
DESIGN AND ART DIRECTION: William Fox Associates
PRODUCTION CO-ORDINATOR: Dorothy Martins
SENIOR EDITOR: Elma Schemenauer

Beginning Skills One

ARTISTS
Ruth Bagshaw—pages 43, 102, 103, 118, 119, 121, 122, 123, 124.
Alan and Lea Daniel in collaboration with J. Merle Smith—pages
16, 17, 18, 19, 22, 23, 30, 32, 33, 34, 35, 36, 37, 38, 39, 40, 41, 58,
59, 60, 61, 62, 63, 64, 65, 66, 67, 70, 71, 74, 75, 76, 77, 80, 81, 86,
87, 88, 89, 90, 91, 94, 95, 116, 117.
Helen Fox—pages 10, 11, 14, 15, 24, 25, 26, 27, 28, 29, 104, 105, 106,
108, 109, 110, 111, 112, 113, 114, 115.
Jack Gray—pages 12, 68, 69, 72, 73, 78, 79, 82, 83, 84, 85.
Vladyana Krykorka—pages 54, 55, 92, 93, 96, 97, 98, 99.
John Mardon—pages 5, 6, 7, 8, 9.
Louise Wiatrowski—pages 42, 44, 45, 46, 47, 48, 49, 50, 51, 52,
53, 56, 57.

ACKNOWLEDGMENTS

"Sheep should not. ..." and "How many cans can a canner can?" from *A Twister of Twists, A Tangler of Tongues* by Alvin
Schwartz. Copyright © 1972 by Alvin Schwartz. Reprinted by permission of J. B. Lippincott Company and Andre
Deutsch Limited.

"Sit Down, Sister" from *More Songs to Grow On* by Beatrice Landeck, arrangement by Florence White. © Copyrighted:
Edward B. Marks Music Corporation. Used by permission.

"Song of the Train" from *Far and Few* by David McCord. Copyright 1952 by David McCord. Reprinted by permission of
Little, Brown and Co. and Curtis Brown Ltd.

"Theophilus, the Thistle Sifter" from *A Rocket in My Pocket,* compiled by Carl Withers.
Copyright 1948 by Carl Withers. Copyright © 1976 by Samuel H. Halperin. Reprinted by permission of
The Bodley Head and Holt, Rinehart and Winston, Publishers.

ISBN 0-02-990820-5
10 9 8 7 6 5 4 3 2 1   82 81 80 79 78

Collier Macmillan Canada, Ltd.
1125B Leslie Street
Don Mills, Ontario M3C 2K2

Manufactured in Canada

Table of Contents

unit one

What are you doing?

I am getting a book.

I am opening a book.

I am closing a book.

I am opening a window.

I am closing a window.

What are you doing?

I am picking up a pencil.

I am holding a pencil.

I am putting down a pencil.

I am opening a door.

I am opening a box.

What are you doing?

I am getting the book.

I am opening the door.

I am closing the door.

I am picking up the box.

I am putting down the box.

I am opening the box.

I am closing the box.

Are you opening the door?

Yes, I am.

Are you getting a book?

Yes, I am.

Are you picking up a pencil?

No, I am not.
I am picking up a book.

Are you opening the box?

No, I am not.
I am closing the box.

What is she doing?

She is catching the ball.

She is hitting the ball.

She is throwing the ball.

She is hitting the ball.

Is she jumping up?
No, she is not.
She is hitting the ball.

She is jumping up.

She is bouncing the ball.

Is she bouncing the ball?
Yes, she is.

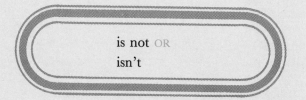

is not OR
isn't

What is he doing?

He is running.

Is he running?
Yes, he is.

He is kicking the ball.

He is falling down.

He is getting up.

He is hitting the ball.

Is he kicking the ball?
No, he is not.
He is hitting the ball.

is not OR

isn't

self test

What is he doing?   What is she doing?

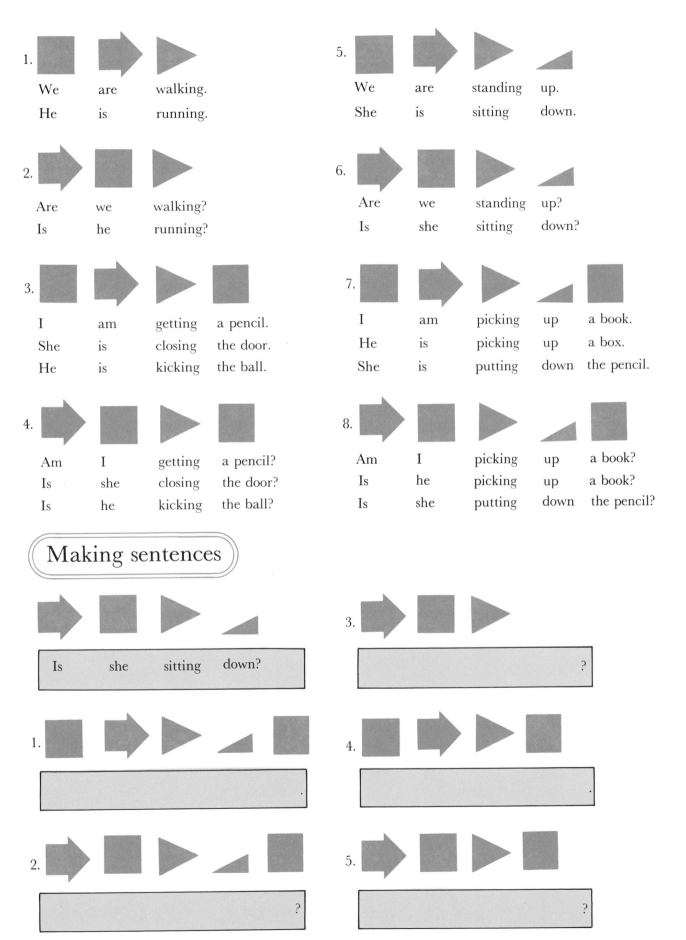

1.
We are walking.
He is running.

2.
Are we walking?
Is he running?

3.
I am getting a pencil.
She is closing the door.
He is kicking the ball.

4.
Am I getting a pencil?
Is she closing the door?
Is he kicking the ball?

5.
We are standing up.
She is sitting down.

6.
Are we standing up?
Is she sitting down?

7.
I am picking up a book.
He is picking up a box.
She is putting down the pencil.

8.
Am I picking up a book?
Is he picking up a book?
Is she putting down the pencil?

Making sentences

Is she sitting down?

3.

1.

4.

2.

5.

unit two

Freddy's feet feel frigid.

Violet's vine violates gravity.

Sam's shirt seems short.

Lizzy's nose looks like a rose.

This is my body.

This is my head.

This is my hair.

This is my nose.

These are my lips.

This is my neck.

These are my shoulders.

This is my chest.

These are my arms.

These are my hands.

This is my waist.

These are my hips.

These are my knees.

These are my legs.

These are my feet.

These are my ears.

These are my eyes.

This is my mouth.

These are my fingers.

These are my toes.

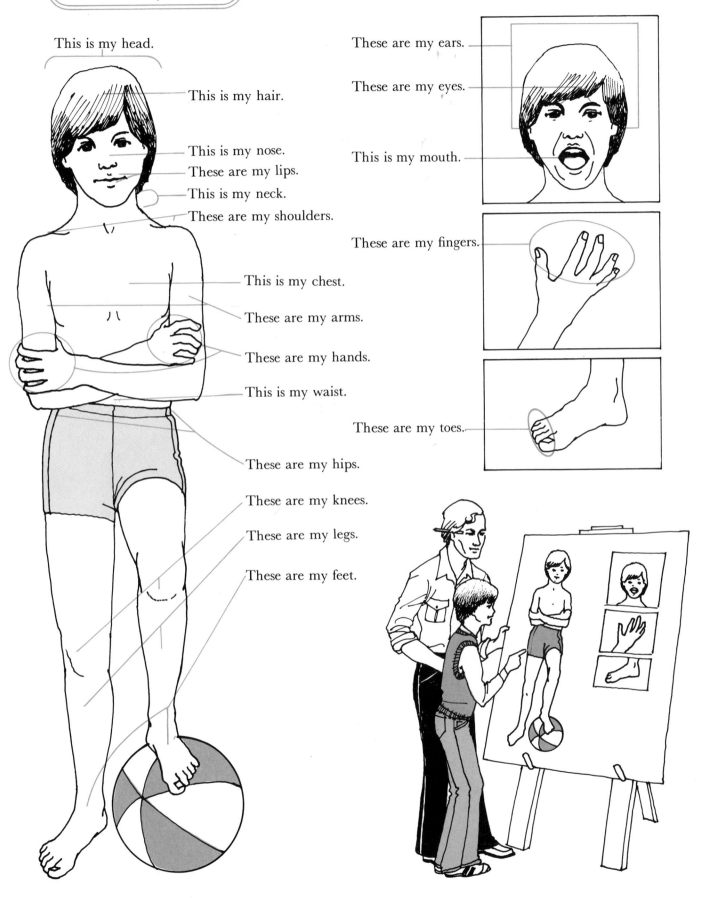

Whose clothes are these?

Whose shoe is this?

This is Leo's shoe. OR
It is his shoe.

Whose socks are these?

These are Leo's socks. OR
They are his socks.

Whose blouse is this?

This is Rose's blouse. OR
It is her blouse.

Whose stockings are these?

These are Kate's stockings. OR
They are her stockings.

Whose purse is this?

This is Rose's purse. OR
It is her purse.

Whose shoe is this?

This is Bonnie's shoe. OR
It is her shoe.

Whose shoes are these?

These are Rose's shoes. OR
They are her shoes.

Whose shirt is this?

This is Bob's shirt. OR
It is his shirt.

Whose sock is this?

This is Bonnie's sock. OR
It is her sock.

Whose pants are these?

These are Bob's pants. OR
They are his pants.

Whose dress is this?

This is Kate's dress. OR
It is her dress.

Whose jacket is this?

This is Leo's jacket. OR
It is his jacket.

Whose belt is this?

This is Bob's belt. OR
It is his belt.

Whose clothes are those?

Leo

Bob

Bonnie

Rose

Kate

Whose coat is that? That is Kate's coat. OR It is her coat.		
Whose underwear is that? That is Bob's underwear. OR It is his underwear.		
Whose jeans are those? Those are Bonnie's jeans. OR They are her jeans.		
Whose sweater is that? That is Rose's sweater. OR It is her sweater.		
Whose skirt is that? That is Rose's skirt. OR It is her skirt.		
Whose shoe is that? That is Leo's shoe. OR It is his shoe.		
Is that Leo's shirt? Yes, it is.		
Is that Leo's shirt? No, it is not.		
Are those Kate's shoes? Yes, they are.		
Are those Kate's shoes? No, they are not.		

is not OR isn't	are not OR aren't

18

Whose clothes are those?

Those are Bob's and Leo's clothes. OR
Those are their shirts.
Those are their socks.

Whose clothes are those?

Those are our clothes. OR
Those are our shirts.
Those are our socks.

What are they doing? *дедают*

1. Lee and Len are sleeping.
2. They are waking up.
3. They are washing their faces.
4. They are brushing their teeth.
5. They are wearing pajamas. *в стуети*
6. They are taking off their pajamas. *снимают*
7. They are combing their hair.
8. They are sitting down.
9. They are eating breakfast. *к-уают   стадашок*
10. They are clearing the table. *cleaning*

What are you doing?

We are putting on our shoes.

Are you putting on your shoes?

Yes, we are.

What are you doing?

We are clearing our desks.

Are you getting your pencils?

No, we are not.
We are clearing our desks.

are not OR
aren't

1.
This   is   my hair.
That   is   Rose's blouse.
Those   are   Bob's pajamas.

2.
Is   this   my hair?
Is   that   Rose's blouse?
Are   those   Bob's pajamas?

3.
Lee and Len are   sleeping.

4.
Are   Lee and Len sleeping?

5.
Lee and Len are   waking up.
They   are   sitting down.

6.
Are   Lee and Len waking up?
Are   they   sitting down?

7.
They   are   wearing   pajamas.
They   are   clearing the table.

8.
Are   they   wearing   pajamas?
Are   they   clearing the table?

9.
We   are   putting on   our shoes.
They   are   taking   off their pajamas.

10.
Are   we   putting on   our shoes?
Are   they   taking   off their pajamas?

Making sentences

Are   those   my shoes?

3.
_____?

1.
_____?

4.
_____.

2.
_____.

5.
_____.

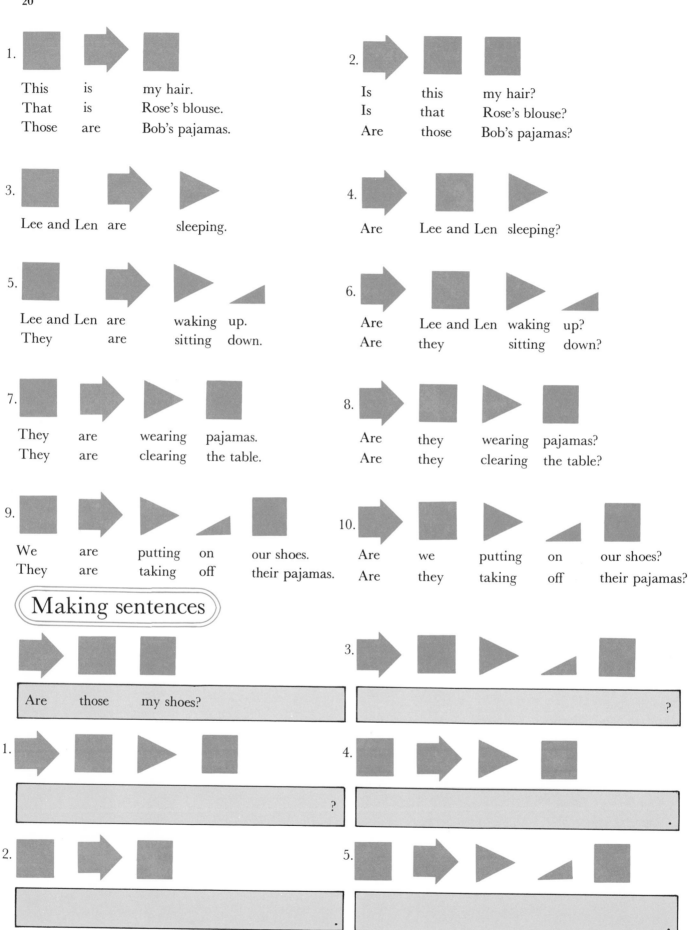

unit three

A

B	I	N	G	O
7	3	2	12	17
4	8	●	20	14
1	6	11	13	19
5	9	15	18	16

B

B	I	N	G	O
9	1	6	16	14
5	4	●	20	11
3	8	10	17	18
7	2	15	13	12

C

B	I	N	G	O
5	4	8	17	14
2	6	●	20	18
7	3	12	15	13
10	9	16	11	19

D

B	I	N	G	O
8	4	9	13	18
1	7	●	19	16
5	3	10	12	14
2	6	17	15	11

22

Where is it?   Where are they?

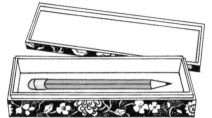

The pencil is in the box.   The pencil is on the box.   The pencil is under the box.

Where is my pencil?   It is in your pocket.

Where is my book?   It is on your desk.

Where are my shoes?   They are under your desk.

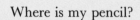

The boy's jacket is on a hook.
His glasses are on his nose.
His hands are on his hips.
His socks are on his feet.
His shoes are on his feet.
He is standing on the floor.

Her glasses are on her nose.
Her book is in her hands.
She is sitting in a chair.

She is sitting on a chair.

self
test

1. What are they doing?

2. Where are they sitting?

3. Where are their feet?

4. Where are their books?

5. Where are their pencils?

Is my purse in your room?

No, it is not.

Is my book on your desk?

Yes, it is.

Are my shoes under your desk?

Yes, they are.

Are my dresses in your closet?

No, they are not.

Sorry!
My purse is under my bed.
My dresses are in my closet.

self test

Is the dress in the closet?
Yes, it is.

Are the shoes in the box?
No, they are not. They are on the box.

here
hear
her

1. Is the purse in the closet?

3. Are her shoes on her feet?

2. Is the shirt on the belt?

4. Are the books on the table?

5. Are the glasses on the floor?

is not OR   are not OR
isn't   aren't

27

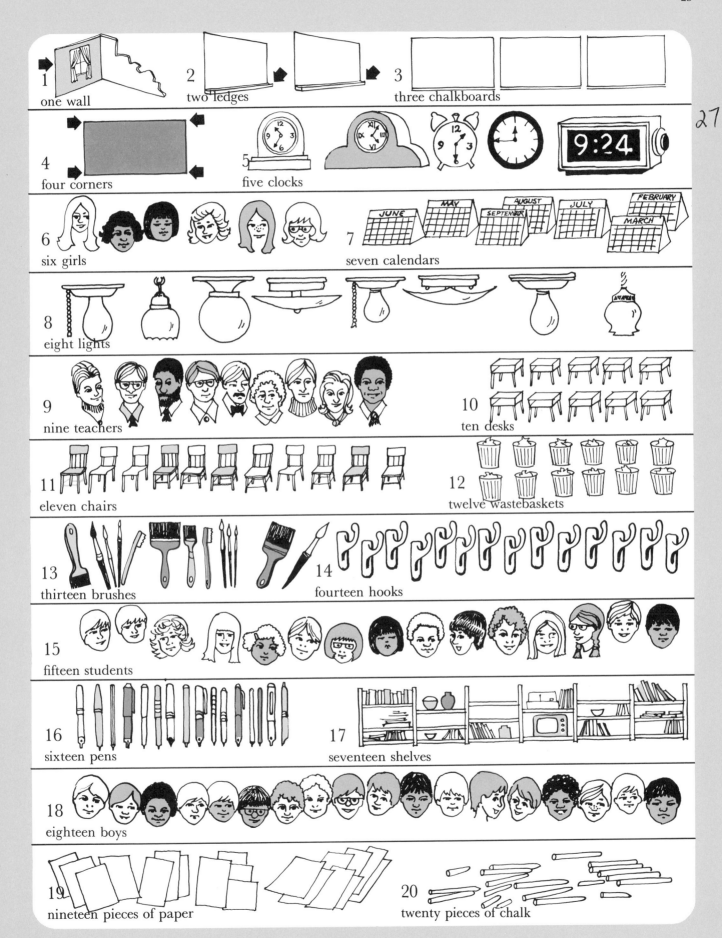

1 one wall

2 two ledges

3 three chalkboards

4 four corners

5 five clocks

6 six girls

7 seven calendars

8 eight lights

9 nine teachers

10 ten desks

11 eleven chairs

12 twelve wastebaskets

13 thirteen brushes

14 fourteen hooks

15 fifteen students

16 sixteen pens

17 seventeen shelves

18 eighteen boys

19 nineteen pieces of paper

20 twenty pieces of chalk

How many?

How many doors are in the room?
There are two doors in the room.

How many windows are in the room?
There are four windows in the room.

How many calendars are in the room?
There is one calendar in the room.

How many desks are in the room?
There are six desks in the room.

How many chairs are in the room?
There is one chair in the room.

How many teachers are in the room?
There is one teacher in the room.

How many students are in the room?
There are three students in the room.

How many books are on the shelves?
There are twelve books on the shelves.

How many pencils are on the teacher's desk?
There are eight pencils on the teacher's desk.

How many books are on the teacher's desk?
There are four books on the teacher's desk.

How many chalkboards are in the room?
There is one chalkboard in the room.

How many hooks are in the room?
There are no hooks in the room.

There are no hooks in the room. OR
There aren't any hooks in the room.

How many?

How many pencils are on the student's desk?

There is one pencil on the student's desk.

How many books are in the student's hands?

There is one book in the student's hands.

How many books are on the student's desk?

There are two books on the student's desk.

How many pencils are on the students' desks?

There are three pencils on the students' desks.

How many books are on the students' desks?

There are four books on the students' desks.

How many books are in the students' hands?

There are two books in the students' hands.

are not OR
aren't

What is in this picture?

Are there any chairs in this picture?
Yes, there are some chairs in this picture.

How many chairs are there?
There are two.

Are there any books in this picture?
Yes, there are some books in this picture.

How many books are there?
There are three.

Are there any students in this picture?
Yes, there are some students in this picture.

How many students are there?
There are four.

Are there any calendars in this picture?
No, there are not any calendars in this picture.

Are there any chalkboards in this picture?
No, there are not any chalkboards in this picture.

is not OR
isn't

What is in this closet?

Are there any dresses in this closet?
Yes, there are some dresses in this closet.

How many dresses are there?
There are three.

Are there any pairs of pants in this closet?
Yes, there are some pairs of pants in this closet.

How many pairs of pants are there?
There are two.

Are there any pairs of shoes in this closet?
Yes, there are some pairs of shoes in this closet.

How many pairs of shoes are there?
There are three.

Are there any pairs of jeans in this closet?
No, there are not any pairs of jeans in this closet.

Is there a coat in this closet?
Yes, there is a coat in this closet. OR
Yes, there is.

Is there a skirt in this closet?
No, there is not a skirt in this closet. OR
No, there is not.

self test

What is in this picture?

There are many students.

There are a few students.

There are many clothes.

There are a few clothes.

There are many pairs of jeans.

There are a few pairs of jeans.

What is in these drawers?

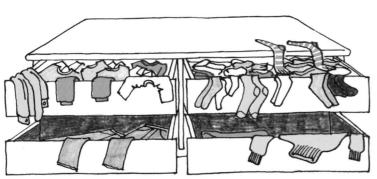

There are many shirts.
There are a few sweaters.
There are many pairs of socks.
There are a few pairs of pajamas.

1. Are there any students in this room?
2. Are there any books on the shelves?
3. Is there a calendar on the wall?
4. Are there any pencils in the box?
5. Is there a ledge in this room?

6. Are there any chalkboards in this room?
7. Are there any brushes in this room?
8. Is there a door in this room?
9. Are there any windows in this room?
10. Is there a teacher on a chair.

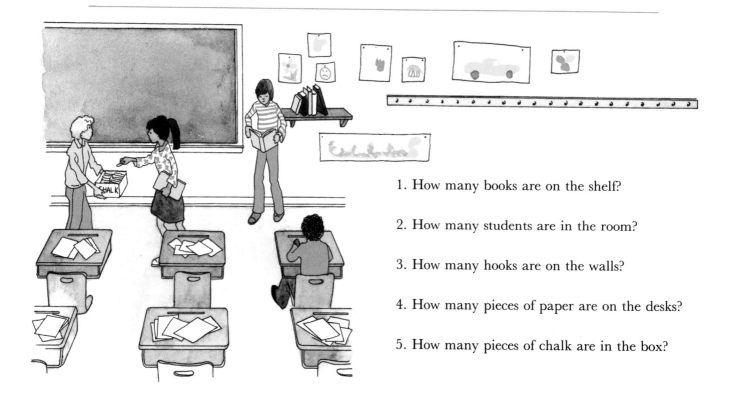

1. How many books are on the shelf?

2. How many students are in the room?

3. How many hooks are on the walls?

4. How many pieces of paper are on the desks?

5. How many pieces of chalk are in the box?

unit four

B	I	N	G	O
1	21	41	61	81
3	24	44	65	83
12	30	●	70	87
15	36	54	77	94
20	40	60	80	99

B	I	N	G	O
2	22	42	62	82
7	23	45	64	86
10	26	●	72	89
14	34	50	75	93
19	39	59	79	98

10 ten	60 sixty	100 one hundred	20 twenty
20 twenty	70 seventy	200 two hundred	21 twenty-one
30 thirty	80 eighty	300 three hundred	22 twenty-two
40 forty	90 ninety	1000 one thousand	23 twenty-three
50 fifty		2000 two thousand	
		3000 three thousand	

100 one hundred	
101 one hundred and one	
102 one hundred and two	
103 one hundred and three	

What time is it?

7:00 a.m.

It is seven o'clock.

7:05 a.m.

It is five minutes after seven.

7:10 a.m.

It is ten minutes after seven.

7:15 a.m.

It is fifteen minutes after seven.

7:40 a.m.

It is seven forty.

7:20 a.m.

It is twenty minutes after seven.

7:45 a.m.

It is seven forty-five.

7:25 a.m.

It is twenty-five minutes after seven.

7:50 a.m.

It is seven fifty.

7:30 a.m.

It is seven-thirty.

7:55 a.m.

It is seven fifty-five.

7:35 a.m.

It is seven thirty-five.

8:00 a.m.

It is eight o'clock.

Good morning.

12:00 p.m.
It is twelve o'clock. OR It is noon.

12:30 p.m.
It is twelve-thirty.

12:35 p.m.
It is twenty-five minutes to one.

12:40 p.m.
It is twenty minutes to one.

12:45 p.m.
It is fifteen minutes to one.

12:50 p.m.
It is ten minutes to one.

12:55 p.m.
It is five minutes to one.

1:00 p.m.
It is one o'clock.

Good afternoon.

Good evening.

6:00 p.m. It is six o'clock.   6:15 p.m. It is a quarter after six.   6:45 p.m. It is a quarter to seven.

Good night.

9:00 p.m. It is nine o'clock.   12:00 a.m. It is twelve o'clock. OR It is midnight.

What are you doing?

What do you do every morning?

I am waking up.

I wake up every morning.

I am washing my face.
I wash my face every morning.

I am brushing my teeth.
I brush my teeth every morning.

I am putting on my clothes.
I put on my clothes every morning.

I am combing my hair.
I comb my hair every morning.

I am eating breakfast.
I eat breakfast every morning.

I am clearing the table.
I clear the table every morning.

Do you wake up every morning?

Yes, I do.

Do you wash your face every morning?

No, I do not.

Do you comb your hair every morning?

Yes, I   comb my hair every morning. OR

Yes, I   do.

Do you wash your hair every morning?

No, I   do not wash my hair every morning. OR

No, I   do not.

do not OR

don't

What does she do every morning?
She wakes up every morning.
She puts on her clothes every morning.

What does she do every afternoon?
She reads a book every afternoon.

What does she do every evening?
She watches TV every evening.

What does he do every morning?
He eats breakfast every morning.

What does he do every afternoon?
He eats lunch every afternoon.

What does he do every evening?
He eats supper every evening.

What do they do every afternoon?
They do their homework every afternoon.

What do they do every evening?
They watch TV every evening.

What do they do every night?
They go to bed every night.

What do you do every afternoon?
We do our homework every afternoon.

What do you do every evening?
We watch TV every evening.

What do you do every night?
We go to bed every night.

What do they do every afternoon?

 1

2

What does she do every evening?

3

 4

What does he do every night?

5

 6

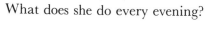

When? OR What time?

When do you eat breakfast? OR
What time do you eat breakfast?

I eat breakfast at 7:15.

When does Bob eat lunch? OR
What time does Bob eat lunch?

He eats lunch at noon.

She does her homework at 3:45.

 3:45

When does Kate do her homework? OR
What time does Kate do her homework?

When do Bob and Kate eat supper? OR
What time do Bob and Kate
eat supper?

Bob and Kate eat supper
at 6 o'clock. OR
They eat supper at 6 o'clock.

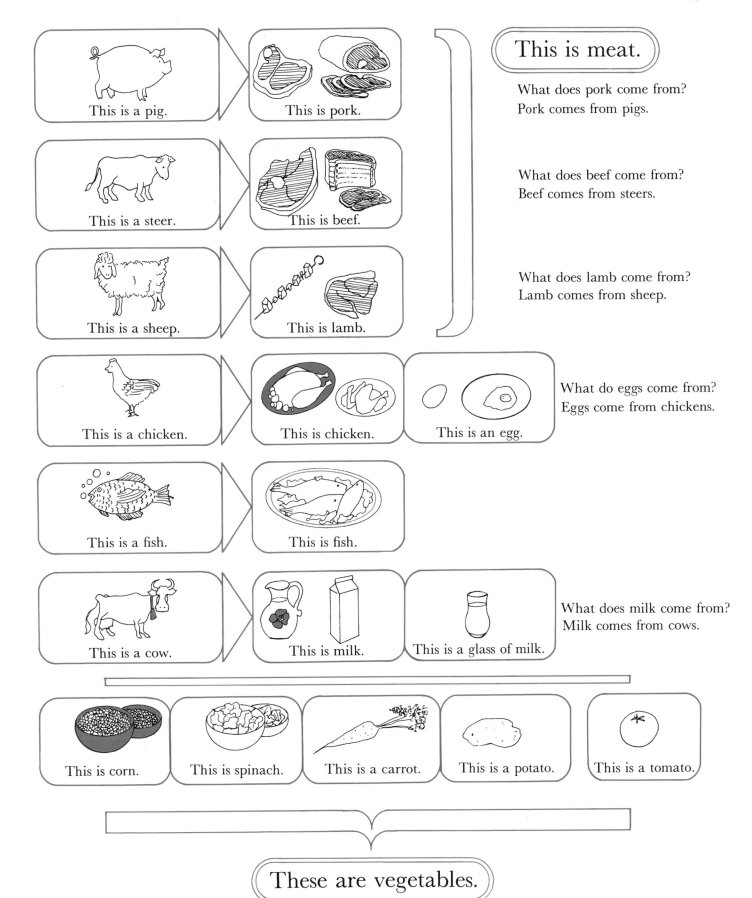

This is a pig. → This is pork.

This is a steer. → This is beef.

This is a sheep. → This is lamb.

This is meat.

What does pork come from?
Pork comes from pigs.

What does beef come from?
Beef comes from steers.

What does lamb come from?
Lamb comes from sheep.

This is a chicken. → This is chicken. This is an egg.

What do eggs come from?
Eggs come from chickens.

This is a fish. → This is fish.

This is a cow. → This is milk. This is a glass of milk.

What does milk come from?
Milk comes from cows.

This is corn. This is spinach. This is a carrot. This is a potato. This is a tomato.

These are vegetables.

38

How many |||||||||||||| do you want?

sausages
eggs
sandwiches
candies
cookies
soft drinks
apples
bananas
oranges

I want one ||||||||||||||. OR

I would like one ||||||||||||||.

sausage
egg
sandwich
candy
cookie
soft drink
apple
banana
orange

How much ||||||||||||||||| do you want?

cereal
soup
toast
juice
milk
water
cake
meat
corn
bread

I want one |||||||||| of ||||||||||||||. OR

I would like one |||||||||| of ||||||||||||||.

bowl	cereal
	soup
piece	toast
	cake
glass	juice
	milk
	water
serving	meat
	corn
slice	bread

I want |||||||||| |||||||||| of ||||||||||. OR

I would like |||||||||| |||||||||| of ||||||||||.

bowls	soup
pieces	toast
glasses	water
servings	meat
slices	bread

Do you want any ||||||||||||?

sausages
eggs
sandwiches
candies
cookies
soft drinks
apples
bananas
oranges

Yes, I want some. OR
Yes, I would like some.

Yes, I want a few. OR
Yes, I would like a few.

Yes, I want a lot. OR
Yes, I would like a lot.

No, I do not want any.

Do you want any ||||||||||||?

cereal
soup
toast
juice
milk
water
cake
meat
corn
bread

Yes, I want some. OR
Yes, I would like some.

Yes, I want a little. OR
Yes, I would like a little.

Yes, I want a lot. OR
Yes, I would like a lot.

No, I do not want any.

do not OR
don't

unit five

◄ She is feeling the box.

She is filling the box. ▶

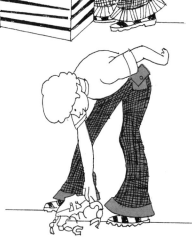

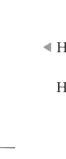

◄ He is picking up the crib.

He is picking up the crab. ▶

Mix a pancake,
Stir a pancake,
   Pop it in the pan;
Fry the pancake,
Toss the pancake,
   Catch it if you can.

What year is it?

  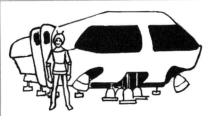

It is 1878. It is 1978. 19   78
nineteen seventy-eight

It is 2078.

What month is it?

It is January.

When is your birthday?   It is June 9th.

What day is today?   What is today's date?

It is Tuesday.

What day is tomorrow?
It is Wednesday.

What day was yesterday?
It was Monday.

Today's date is January 15th. OR
It is January 15th. OR
It is the 15th.

What is tomorrow's date?

Tomorrow's date is January 16th. OR
It is January 16th. OR
It is the 16th.

1st	**first**	1	one	6th	six**th**	6	six	13th	thir**teenth**	13	thirteen
2nd	**second**	2	two	7th	seven**th**	7	seven	20th	twent**ieth**	20	twenty
3rd	**third**	3	three	8th	eigh**th**	8	eight	21st	twenty-**first**	21	twenty-one
4th	four**th**	4	four	9th	nin**th**	9	nine	30th	thirt**ieth**	30	thirty
5th	fi**fth**	5	five	10th	ten**th**	10	ten	31st	thirty-**first**	31	thirty-one

week

Monday	Tuesday	Wednesday	Thursday	Friday	Saturday	Sunday

weekdays   weekend

Where are they going now?   Where do they go every day?

She is going to school now.
She goes to school every weekday.

He is going home now.
He goes home every day.

He is going home now.
He goes home every day.

She is going to the grocery store now.
She goes to the grocery store every Tuesday.

He is going to the supermarket now.
He goes to the supermarket every Saturday.

She is going to the drugstore now.
She goes to the drugstore every Friday.

They are going to the library now.
They go to the library every week.

They are going to a restaurant now.
They go to a restaurant every weekend.

They are going to a gas station now.
They go to a gas station every week.

Where are they going now? Where do they go every week?

They are going to a movie now.
They go to a movie every Sunday.

They are going to a concert now.
They go to a concert every weekend.

They are going to a concert now.
They go to a concert every weekend.

They are going to a basketball game now.
They go to a basketball game every Friday.

They are going to a soccer game now.
They go to a soccer game every Saturday.

They are going to a hockey game now.
They go to a hockey game every weekend.

They are going to a baseball game now.
They go to a baseball game every Thursday.

She is going to a swimming meet now.
She goes to a swimming meet every Saturday.

They are going to a party now.
They go to a party every weekend.

How do you get to school?

Lucy

I always walk.
First I go up Second Street for two blocks.
Then I turn right.
I go east along Champlain Avenue for a block.
Then I cross Champlain Avenue.
Then I am at school.

Ken

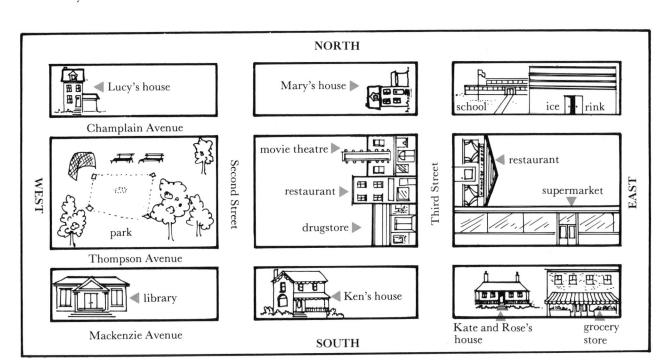

NORTH

Lucy's house

Champlain Avenue

Mary's house

school   ice   rink

WEST

movie theatre

restaurant

drugstore

park

Thompson Avenue

Second Street

restaurant

supermarket

Third Street

EAST

library

Mackenzie Avenue

Ken's house

SOUTH

Kate and Rose's house

grocery store

How does Lucy get to school?

She usually walks.
She goes east along Champlain Avenue for two blocks.
Then she is at school.

How do you get to the movie theatre?

Mary

Rose

Kate

We usually walk.
First we go west along Mackenzie Avenue.
Then we turn right.
We go north up Third Street for two blocks.
Then we cross Third Street.
Then we are at the movie theatre.

How do you get to school?

self test

I usually ||||||||||||||||||||||||||||||||||||||||||||||||.

First I |||||||||||||||||||||| for ||||||||||||||||||||||||||||||.

Then I turn |||||||||||||||||||||||||||||||||.

I go |||||||||||||||||||||||||||||||||||||||||

for ||||||||||||||||||||||||||||||||||||||||||.

The girl is going out.
The boy is coming in.

She is going to school.

He is coming to school.

How does she get to school?

How does he get to school?

She always walks.

She usually goes by bus. OR
By bus.

He sometimes goes by car. OR
By car.

He sometimes goes by taxi. OR
By taxi.

She sometimes goes by truck. OR
By truck.

He always goes by plane. OR
By plane.

He usually comes by train. OR By train.

She always comes by boat. OR By boat.

He always rides his bicycle.

She usually rides her horse.

Does he go to school by bus?

No, he does not.
He goes by plane.

Does she walk to school?

No, she does not.
She rides her horse to school.

Does she walk to school?

Yes, she walks to school. OR
Yes, she does.

does not OR
doesn't

Do they go to school by train?

No, they do not.
They go to school by bus.

Do they go to school by boat?

Yes, they go to school by boat. OR
Yes, they do.

do not OR
don't

unit six

◄He is holding a pig.
He is holding a peg.►

◄She is sitting on a pole.
She is sitting on a bowl.►

Peter Piper picked a peck of pickled peppers;
A peck of pickled peppers Peter Piper picked.
If Peter Piper picked a peck of pickled peppers,
Where's the peck of pickled peppers Peter Piper picked?

My family

I have two brothers.

This is my younger brother.

He is my baby brother.

This is my older brother.

This is my father.

This is my mother.

I have two sisters.

This is my twin sister.

This is my younger sister.

My relatives

I have many cousins.

Those are my cousins.

Those are my aunts.

Those are my uncles.

Those are my grandmothers.

Those are my grandfathers.

Are these your relatives?

Yes, they are.
These are my grandparents.
These are my uncles and aunts.
These are my cousins.

Is this your father?

It is my stepfather.

Are these your parents?

These are my foster parents.
This is Shirley and this is Victor.

How old are you?

I am twelve years old. OR
I am twelve.
My older sister is sixteen years old. OR
My older sister is sixteen.
My younger sisters are eight years old
and six years old. OR
My younger sisters are eight and six.
My baby brother is two years old. OR
My baby brother is two.

I am older than you are. OR
I am older than you.

I am younger than you are. OR
I am younger than you.

My grandfather is eighty years old.
He is the oldest person in our family.

My baby brother is two years old.
He is the youngest person in our family.

self test

1. How old are you?

2. How many brothers do you have?
   How old are they?

3. How many sisters do you have?
   How old are they?

4. Do you have any older brothers?
   Do you have any younger brothers?

5. Do you have any older sisters?
   Do you have any younger sisters?

6. Who is the oldest person in your family?
   Who is the youngest person in your family?

55

How tall are you?

I am 151 cm tall.

I am 153 cm tall.
I am taller than you are. OR
I am taller than you. OR
I am taller.

100 cm	one hundred centimetres
101 cm	one hundred one centimetres
150 cm	one hundred fifty centimetres
151 cm	one hundred fifty-one centimetres
151.5 cm	one hundred fifty-one point five centimetres
150.9 cm	one hundred fifty point nine centimetres

Which one is taller?

Which boy is taller?

The first boy is taller than the second boy. OR
The first boy is taller. OR
The first one is taller.

Which girl is taller?

The second girl is taller than the first girl. OR
The second girl is taller. OR
The second one is taller.

Which one is the tallest?

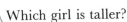

Which tree is the tallest?

The second tree is the tallest. OR
The second one is the tallest.

Which boy is the tallest?

The third boy is the tallest. OR
The third one is the tallest.

Which girl is the tallest?

The fifth girl is the tallest. OR
The fifth one is the tallest.

How high is it?

This fence is 104 cm high.

This fence is 99 cm high.

The first fence is higher than the second fence.

Which one is higher?

Which shelf is higher?

The top shelf is higher than the bottom shelf. OR

The top shelf is higher. OR

The top one is higher.

Which hill is higher?

The first hill is higher than the second hill. OR

The first hill is higher. OR

The first one is higher.

Which boy is higher?

The first boy is higher than the second boy. OR

The first boy is higher. OR

The first one is higher.

How long is it?

This pencil is 14 cm long.

This pencil is 10 cm long.

The first pencil is longer than the second pencil.

Which one is longer?

Which girl's hair is longer?

The first girl's hair is longer than the second girl's hair. OR

The first girl's hair is longer. OR

The first one's hair is longer.

Which rope is longer?

The second rope is longer than the first rope. OR

The second rope is longer. OR

The second one is longer.

Which line is longer?

The first line is longer than the second line. OR

The first line is longer. OR

The first one is longer.

Which fence is longer?

The first fence is longer than the second fence. OR

The first fence is longer. OR

The first one is longer.

How thick is it?

This book is 5 cm thick.  This book is 2 cm thick.

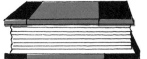

The first book is thicker than the second book.

Which one is thicker?

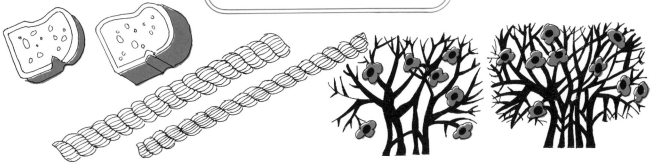

Which slice of bread is thicker?

The second slice of bread is thicker than the first slice of bread. OR

The second slice of bread is thicker. OR

The second one is thicker.

Which rope is thicker?

The first rope is thicker than the second rope. OR

The first rope is thicker. OR

The first one is thicker.

Which bush is thicker?

The second bush is thicker than the first bush. OR

The second bush is thicker. OR

The second one is thicker.

How wide is it?

This door is 84 cm wide. This door is 50 cm wide.

The first door is wider than the second door.

Which one is wider?

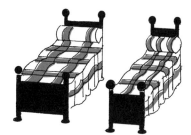  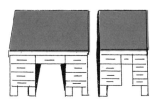

Which bed is wider?

The first bed is wider than the second bed. OR

The first bed is wider. OR

The first one is wider.

Which foot is wider?

The second foot is wider than the first foot. OR

The second foot is wider. OR

The second one is wider.

Which desk is wider?

The first desk is wider than the second desk. OR

The first desk is wider. OR

The first one is wider.

How big is it?

This piece of paper is 4 cm by 2.5 cm.

This piece of paper is 2.5 cm by 1 cm.

The first piece of paper is bigger than the second piece of paper.

Which one is bigger?

Which ball is bigger?

The soccer ball is bigger than the baseball. OR
The soccer ball is bigger.

Which hand is bigger?

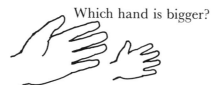

The boy's hand is bigger than the baby's hand. OR
The boy's hand is bigger.

Which box is bigger?

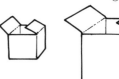

The second box is bigger than the first box. OR
The second box is bigger.

self test

long

Which rope is longer?
The first rope is longer than the second rope.

wide

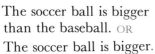

Which car is the widest?
The fourth car is the widest.

high
①

tall
②

thick
③

big
④

long
⑤

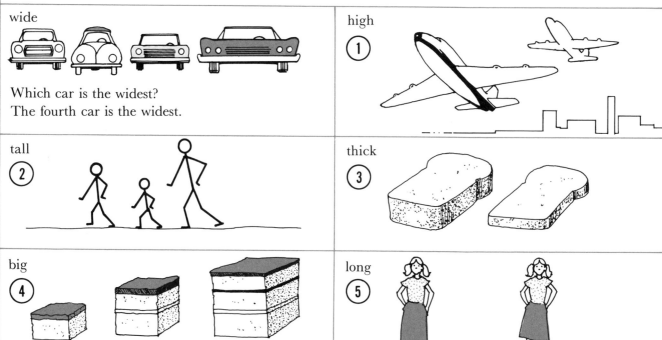

Which boy is taller?
Neither. They are the same height.

Which rope is the longest?
None. They are the same length.

 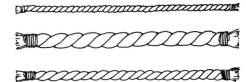

Which belt is wider?
Neither. They are the same width.

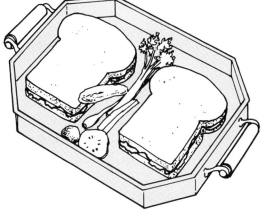

Which sandwich is thicker?
Neither. They are the same thickness.

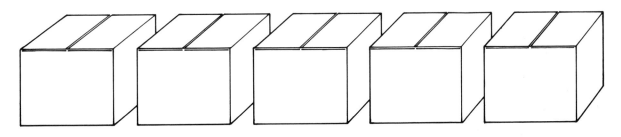

Which box is the biggest?
None. They are the same size.

unit seven

◀ Sheep should not sleep in a shoe.

Sheep should sleep in a shed. ▶

> should not OR
> shouldn't

How many cans can a canner can
If a canner can can cans?
A canner can can as many cans
As a canner can
If a canner can can cans.

What do you see in this picture?

I see **the moon**. 1

Where is **the moon**? 2

It is in the sky. OR
The moon is in the sky.

I see **a star**. 1

Where is **the star**? 2

It is in the sky. OR
The star is in the sky.

What do you see in this picture?

I see the sun.

I see some clouds. OR
I see three clouds.

I see a girl.

I see some fish. OR
I see three fish.

I see a house.

I see some flowers. OR
I see eleven flowers.

I see a lake.

I see a truck.

I see some planes. OR
I see two planes.

I see a tree.

I see a pig.

I see some cars. OR
I see four cars.

I see some birds. OR
I see six birds.

I see a nest.

I see a road.

I see a dog.

Where is the girl?
She is in a cloud.

Where should she be?
She should be on the ground.

Where is the sun?
It is in the sky.

Should it be in the sky?
Yes, it should be in the sky. OR
Yes, it should.

Should the cars be on the road?
Yes, they should be on the road. OR
Yes, they should.

Should the pig be in the tree?
No, it should not be in the tree. OR
No, it should not.

Should the fish be in the sky?
No, they should not be in the sky. OR
No, they should not.

Where is the nest?
It is on the car.

Where should it be?
It should be in the tree.

Where are the flowers?
They are on the roof.

Where should they be?
They should be in the ground.

Where are the planes?
They are in the lake. OR
They are in the water.

Where should they be?
They should be in the sky.

should not OR

shouldn't

64

self test

What is wrong?

His shirt is on backwards. OR
His shirt is backwards.

Her head is on upside down. OR
Her head is upside down.

①

②

③

④

⑤

Should he clear the table?
Yes, he should.

Should she wash her face?
Yes, she should.

Should she put on her shoes now?
No, she should not.

Should he open the door?
No, he should not.

Should you put on your coat?
Yes, I should.

Should you eat this bread?
No, I should not.

should not OR
shouldn't

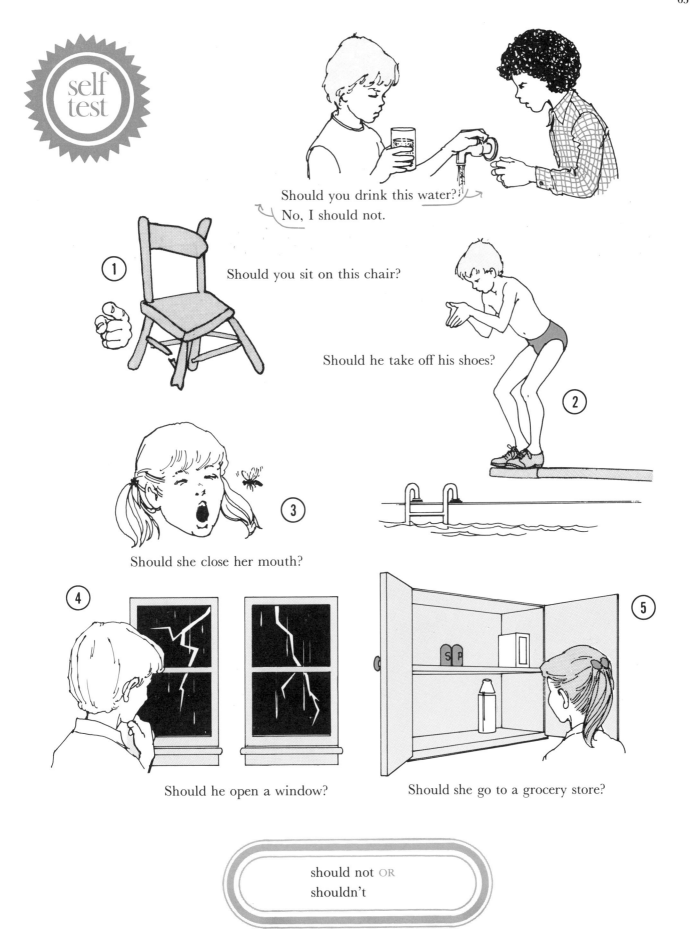

self test

Should you drink this water?
No, I should not.

① Should you sit on this chair?

Should he take off his shoes?

②

③ Should she close her mouth?

④ Should he open a window?

⑤ Should she go to a grocery store?

should not OR
shouldn't

66

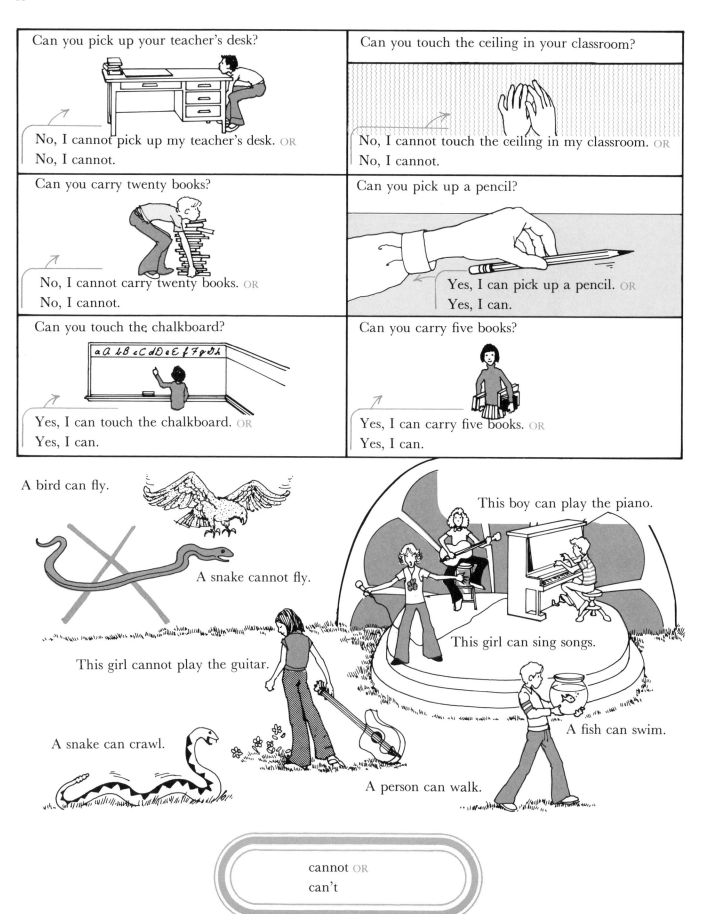

Can you pick up your teacher's desk?

No, I cannot pick up my teacher's desk. OR
No, I cannot.

Can you touch the ceiling in your classroom?

No, I cannot touch the ceiling in my classroom. OR
No, I cannot.

Can you carry twenty books?

No, I cannot carry twenty books. OR
No, I cannot.

Can you pick up a pencil?

Yes, I can pick up a pencil. OR
Yes, I can.

Can you touch the chalkboard?

Yes, I can touch the chalkboard. OR
Yes, I can.

Can you carry five books?

Yes, I can carry five books. OR
Yes, I can.

A bird can fly.

A snake cannot fly.

This girl cannot play the guitar.

A snake can crawl.

This boy can play the piano.

This girl can sing songs.

A person can walk.

A fish can swim.

cannot OR

can't

self test

Can this boy play soccer?

No, he cannot play soccer. OR
No, he cannot.

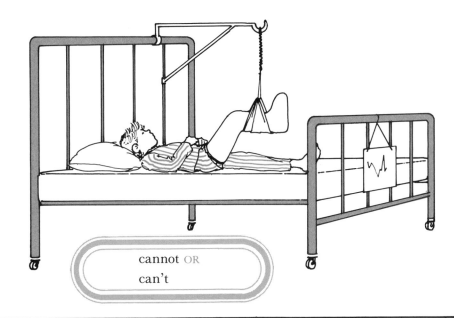

cannot OR

can't

① Can this fish play the piano?
Can a fish really play the piano?

② Can this bird fly?

③ Can this girl open this door?

④ Can a dog play the guitar?

⑤ Can a snake fly?

What is it made of?

What is your dress made of?

It is made of cloth.

What are your shoes made of?

They are made of leather.

What is your desk made of?

It is made of wood.

What is your purse made of?

It is made of vinyl.

What is your pen made of?

It is made of plastic.

What is your wristwatch made of?

It is made of metal.

What is your sweater made of?

It is made of acrylic.

68

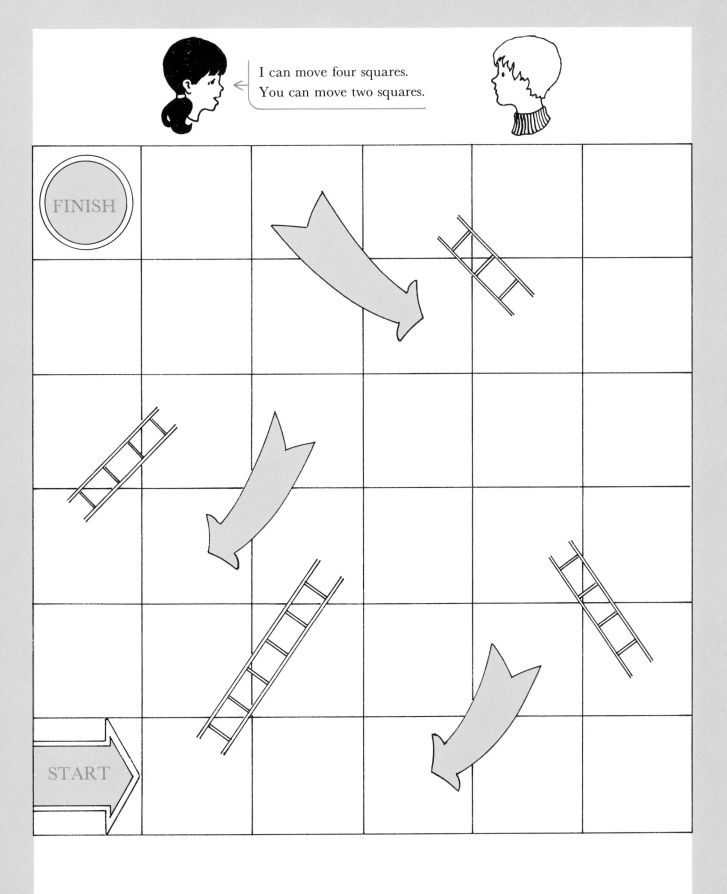

unit eight

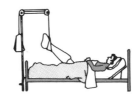

▲ She has two decks.

▲ The man cannot walk.

▲ Do not pinch me.

▼ She has two ducks.

▼ The men cannot walk.

▼ Do not punch me.

cannot OR

can't

Betty Botter bought some butter,
But, she said, the butter's bitter;
If I put it in my batter
It will make my batter bitter.
But a bit of better butter,
That would make my batter better.

So she bought a bit of butter
Better than her bitter butter,
And she put it in her batter
And the batter was not bitter.
So it was better Betty Botter
Bought a bit of better butter.

When do you usually wake up?

I usually wake up at 7:00.

When do you eat breakfast?

I usually eat breakfast at 7:30.
I wake up before I eat breakfast. OR
I eat breakfast after I wake up.

Paul puts on his socks.
Then Paul puts on his shoes.

He puts on his socks before he puts on his shoes. OR
He puts on his shoes after he puts on his socks.

These students take off their coats.
Then they sit down.

These students take off their coats
before they sit down. OR
These students sit down after they
take off their coats.

abcdefg
hijklmn
opqrstu
vwxyz

Does C come before B?

No, C does not come before B. OR
No, it does not.
C comes after B.

Does E come after F?

No, E does not come after F. OR
No, it does not.
E comes before F.

1 2 3 4 5
6 7 8 9 10

Does 2 come before 8?

Yes, 2 comes before 8. OR
Yes, it does.

Does 7 come after 6?

Yes, 7 comes after 6. OR
Yes, it does.

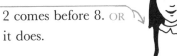

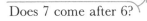

does not OR
doesn't

Carol's class schedule

	Monday, Wednesday, Friday	Tuesday, Thursday
9:00 a.m.	French language	French language
10:00 a.m.	recess	recess
10:15 a.m.	mathematics	mathematics
11:00 a.m.	English language	English language
12:00 p.m.	lunch	lunch
1:00 p.m.	social studies	science
1:45 p.m.	music	art
2:15 p.m.	recess	recess
2:30 p.m.	physical education	health education
3:15 p.m.	home economics	industrial arts

Carol has music before she has recess every Monday, Wednesday, and Friday.
Carol has health education after she has recess every Tuesday and Thursday.

What do you see in this picture?

I see it.

I see it.

I see it.

I see it.

I see it.

I see them.

I see her.

I see her.

I see him.

I see him.

He sees me.

I see you.

I see you.

I see myself.

I see myself.

A Detective Story

It is eating me up.

It ate me up.

First I came in the room.
Then I grabbed the girl and ate her up.

What happened?

My child disappeared.

Look at this. I see a footprint.
It is not a human being's footprint.
It is a monster's footprint.

Let's find that monster.
Let's save your child.

How can we save your child?

We can tickle the monster.

I saw a footprint.
It was not a human being's footprint.
It was a monster's footprint.
We found the monster.
We tickled it.
We saved you.

What happened?

The girl closed the door.
Then she opened the window.
A monster came in the room.
It grabbed the girl.
It ate her up.

What is he doing?	What did he do?
He is carrying twenty books.	He carried twenty books.
He is clearing his desk.	He cleared his desk.
He is touching the ceiling.	He touched the ceiling.
He is walking to school.	He walked to school.
He is washing his socks.	He washed his socks.
He is picking up his desk.	He picked up his desk.

What is she doing?

What did she do?

She is sitting down.

She sat down.

She is putting on her shoes.

She put on her shoes.

She is going to school by plane.

She went to school by plane.

She is taking off her sweater.

She took off her sweater.

What did he do?

He opened the door.   Then he closed it.

What did she do?

She washed her hair.   Then she combed it.

What did they do?
They got their books.   Then they opened them.

What did he do?
He got some sandwiches.   Then he ate them.

First take off your shoes.
Then put your shoes on your hands.

He took off his shoes.
Then he put them on his hands.

He	picked up	a book.		Did	he	pick up	a book?
He	picked	a book up.		Did	he	pick	a book up?
He	picked	it	up.	Did	he	pick	it	up?

Did he pick up a book? OR
Did he pick a book up?

Yes, he picked it up.

Did he put on his shirt? OR
Did he put his shirt on?

Yes, he put it on.

Did he take off his belt? OR
Did he take his belt off?

Yes, he took it off.

Yes, she picked them up.

Did she pick up two pencils? OR
Did she pick two pencils up?

Did she put on her shoes? OR
Did she put her shoes on?

Yes, she put them on.

Did he take off his jeans? OR
Did he take his jeans off?

No, he did not take them off.
He took off his socks. OR
He took his socks off.

did not OR
didn't

Please turn on the lights. OR
Please turn the lights on. OR
Please turn them on.

Please turn off the lights. OR
Please turn the lights off. OR
Please turn them off.

Please turn on the TV. OR
Please turn the TV on. OR
Please turn it on.

Please turn off the TV. OR
Please turn the TV off. OR
Please turn it off.

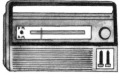

radio

stereo

oven

water

unit nine

A tutor who tooted the flute

A **Tut**or who **toot**ed the **flute**
Tried to **teach** two young **toot**ers to **toot**;
Said the **two** to the **Tut**or,
"Is it **hard**er to **toot**, or
To **tut**or two **toot**ers to **toot**?"

84

1 Does this cake smell good or bad?
Does it feel hard or soft?

2 Does this boy's hair look light or dark?
Do his clothes look light or dark?
Do his shoes look shiny or dull?

3 Do these clothes look wet or dry?
Do they look clean or dirty?

4 Does the road look bumpy or smooth?
Do the tires on the car look hard or soft?

tire

5 Does this person look hot or cold?

How does it feel?
How does it look?
How does it smell?

1 a zipper

2 a brick wall

3 sandpaper

4 a mirror

5 a slipper

6 wood

7 a cake

8 an ice cube

9 a kitten

10 cardboard

11 fire

These are plants.

This is a tree.
A tree is a plant.
It has branches.
It has leaves.
It has a trunk.
Bark is on the trunk.
It has roots.

This is a flower.
A flower is a plant.
It has petals.
It has leaves.
It has a stem.
It has roots.

This is a leaf.

These are leaves.

This is grass.
Grass is a plant.

This is a blade of grass.   It has roots.

These are minerals.

This is a stone.

This is a rock.

This is soil.

Plants grow in the soil.
Stones and rocks are in the soil.

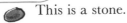

Touch some leaves.
How do they feel?
Do they feel rough or smooth?

These leaves do not feel rough.
They feel smooth.

How do they look?
Do they look dark or light?
Do they look shiny or dull?

These leaves do not look light.
They look dark.
They do not look dull.
They look shiny.

How do they smell?
Do they smell good or bad?
These leaves have no smell.

do not. OR
don't.

This jacket is made of cloth.

What kind of jacket is that?

It is a cloth jacket.

This jacket is made of leather.

What kind of jacket is that?

It is a leather jacket.

These shoes are made of canvas.

What kind of shoes are those?

They are canvas shoes.

This bookcase is made of wood.

What kind of bookcase is that?

It is a wooden bookcase.

These walls are made of concrete block.

What kind of walls are those?

They are concrete block walls.

These stairs are made of concrete.

What kind of stairs are those?

They are concrete stairs.

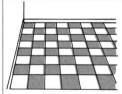

This floor is made of tile.

What kind of floor is that?

It is a tile floor.

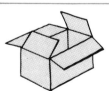

This box is made of cardboard.

What kind of box is that?

It is a cardboard box.

This jar is made of glass.

What kind of jar is that?

It is a glass jar.

self test

What kind of bottle is this?
It is a glass bottle.

1.What kind of stairs are these?

2.What kind of shoes are these?

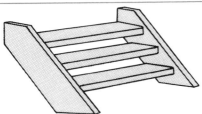

3.What kind of telephone is this?

4.What kind of house is this?

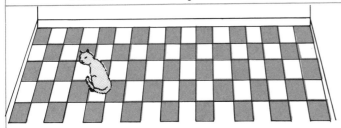

5.What kind of floor is this?

6.What kind of box is this?

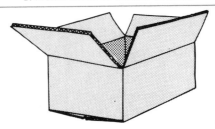

7.What kind of doghouse is this?

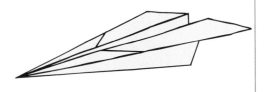

8.What kind of airplane is this?

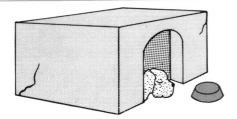

9.What kind of fence is this?

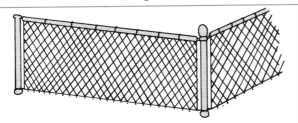

10.What kind of monsters are these?

This room is too dark. I cannot see.

This bread is too hard. I cannot eat it.

This road is too bumpy. We cannot ride on it.

This bowl is too hot. I cannot hold it.

This bed is too hard. I cannot sleep in it.

This dress is too long. I cannot wear it.

This shelf is too high. I cannot reach it.

This book is too thick. I cannot put it in my schoolbag.

These pants are too short. I cannot wear them.

This rope is too short. I cannot use it.

This bed is too narrow. I cannot sleep in it.

This doorway is too narrow. I cannot walk through it.

This space is too narrow. I cannot walk through it.

This car is too wide. I cannot drive it through this street.

This table is too wide. We cannot carry it through this doorway.

cannot OR can't

These jeans are too short.
I cannot wear them.

self test

1

2

3

4

5

6

7

8

9

10

cannot OR
can't

unit ten

Song of the train

Clickety-clack,
Wheels on the track,
This is the way
They begin the attack:
Click-ety-clack,
Click-ety-clack,
Click-ety, **clack**-ety,
Click-ety
Clack.

Clickety-clack,
Over the crack,
Faster and faster
The song of the track:
Clickety-clack,
Clickety-clack,
Clickety-clackety,
Clackety
Clack.

Riding in front,
Riding in back,
Everyone hears
The song of the track:
Clickety-clack,
Clickety-clack,
Clickety, **clickety,**
Clackety
Clack.

This is a new shirt.
This is an old shirt.

These are new shoes.
These are old shoes.

This is a big hamburger.
This is a little hamburger.

These are big dogs.
These are little dogs.

This is a fat man.
This is a thin man.

These are fat babies.
These are thin babies.

This is a thick rope.
This is a thin rope.

These are thick books.
These are thin books.

This is a heavy box.
This is a light box.

These are heavy coats.
These are light coats.

This is a wet towel.
This is a dry towel.

These are wet cats.
These are dry cats.

This is a sharp knife.
This is a dull knife.

These are sharp knives.
These are dull knives.

These are sharp scissors.
These are dull scissors.

This is a straight line.
This is a crooked line.

What is the matter?

This rope is too thin.
We have to get a thicker one.

This chair is too heavy.
I have to get a lighter one.

This cat is too thin.
We have to find a fatter cat.

This jacket is too small.
I have to get a bigger one.

These knives are too dull.
I have to get some sharper ones.

SNACKS

CIRCUS

This sign is old.
We have to make a new one.

That table is wet.
We have to find a dry one.

That letter **I** is crooked.
You have to make a straight one.

| What did they do? | What did he do? | What did she do? |

He got a lighter chair.

They got a thicker rope.

She got some sharper knives.

She got a bigger jacket.

They found a fatter cat.

SNACKS

CIRCUS

He made a straight letter **I**.

They found a dry table.

They made a new sign.

94

What is the matter?

What does he have to do?   What did he do?

find   That dog is too fat.
The boy has to find a thinner one.

He found a thinner one.

1 make

2 find

3 get

What does she have to do?   What did she do?

What does he have to do?   What did he do?

She has to find her shoes.

She found her shoes.

He has to comb his hair.

He combed his hair.

1

2

3

4

5

What do you want to do?

I want to read.

I want to sleep.

I do not want to jump.

I want to run.

I want to sing.

I do not want to stand up.

I do not want to sit down.

I want to turn the lights off.

I want to turn the lights on.

I want to look out the window.

I want to look in this drawer.

I want to write on the chalkboard.

I want to talk to my teacher.

I want to go to the bathroom.

I want to listen to the radio.

do not OR

don't

What does she want to do?

She wants to kick the ball.

She wants to catch the ball.

She wants to hit the ball.

What does he want to do?

◄ He wants to go out.
He wants to come in. ➤

What do you want to do?

◄ We want to watch TV.
We do not want to go home. ➤

What do they want to do?

They want to turn your radio off.

They want to turn the water on.

do not OR
don't

Do you want to turn on the water?

No, I do not want to turn it on. OR
No, I do not.
I want to turn it off.

Do you want to watch TV?

Yes, I want to watch TV. OR
Yes, I do.

Does he want to go out?

No, he does not want to go out. OR
No, he does not.

Does he want to stay in the house?

Yes, he wants to stay in the house. OR
Yes, he does.

self test

do not OR   does not OR
don't   doesn't

What is the length of this line?

This line is 2.3 cm long. OR
This line is two point three centimetres long. OR

This line is 23 mm long. OR
This line is twenty-three millimetres long.

What is the width of this window?

This window is 1.1 m wide. OR
This window is one point one metres wide.

What is the height of this table?

This table is 1 m high. OR
This table is one metre high.

Measuring things

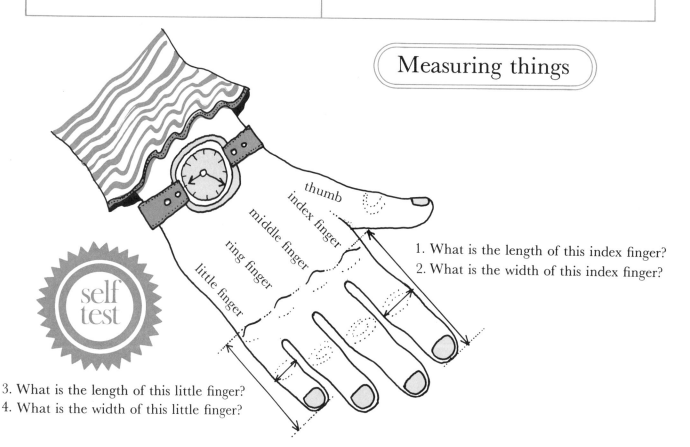

self test

1. What is the length of this index finger?
2. What is the width of this index finger?

3. What is the length of this little finger?
4. What is the width of this little finger?

5. What is the length of your thumb?
6. What is the length of your ring finger?
7. What is the width of your ring finger?

8. What is the length of your desk?
9. What is the height of your desk?
10. What is the width of your desk?

Are they the same or different?

Victor and Scott are the same height.

Are Victor and Scott the same height?
Yes, they are.

Judy and Gloria weigh the same.

Do Judy and Gloria weigh the same?
Yes, they do.

Are Gloria and Victor the same height?

No, they are not.
They are different heights.
Gloria is taller than Victor.

Do Scott and Judy weigh the same?

No, they do not.
They weigh different amounts.
Scott is heavier than Judy.

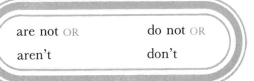

are not OR	do not OR
aren't	don't

unit eleven

Sit down Sister, sit down Brother

Oh, won't you sit down, Sister? I can't sit down. Oh, won't you
Brother

sit down, Sister? I can't sit down. Oh, won't you sit down, Sister? I
Brother Brother

Fine

can't sit down, 'Cause I just got to Heaven, Have to look a — round.

Who are those children dressed in red? They have to be the children that

D.C.al Fine

Mo ses led.

Sit down Sister, sit down Brother

Girls	Boys
Oh, won't you sit down, Brother ?	I can't sit down.
Oh, won't you sit down, Brother ?	I can't sit down.
Oh, won't you sit down, Brother ?	I can't sit down,
	'Cause I just got to Heaven, Have to look around.
Who are those children dressed in red?	They have to be the children that Moses led.
Who are those children dressed in white?	They have to be the children of the Israelite.
Oh, won't you sit down, Brother ?	I can't sit down.
Oh, won't you sit down, Brother ?	I can't sit down.
Oh, won't you sit down, Brother?	I can't sit down. 'Cause I just got to Heaven, Have to look around.

Boys	Girls
Oh, won't you sit down, Sister?	I can't sit down.
Oh, won't you sit down, Sister?	I can't sit down.
Oh, won't you sit down, Sister?	I can't sit down,
	'Cause I just got to Heaven, Have to look around.
Who are those children dressed in red?	They have to be the children that Moses led.
Who are those children dressed in·white?	They have to be the children of the Israelite.
Oh, won't you sit down, Sister?	I can't sit down.
Oh, won't you sit down, Sister?	I can't sit down.
Oh, won't you sit down, Sister?	I can't sit down. 'Cause I just got to Heaven, Have to look around.

will not OR
won't

1.

He   is   writing   his name.
He   should   write   his name.
He   can   write   his name.
He   will   write   his name.

2.

Is   he   writing   his name?
Should   he   write   his name?
Can   he   write   his name?
Will   he   write   his name?

3.

He   writes   his name.

4.

Does   he   write   his name?

We have only two.
We have to get another one.
We have only one.
We have to get two more.
We have a few.
We have to get some more.
We have only two pieces.
We have to get another piece.
We have only one piece.
We have to get two more pieces.
We have a little.
We have to get some more.

How many pencils do we have?
How many books do we have?
How many brushes do we have?
How much chalk do we have?
How much paper do we have?
How much paint do we have?

We have a lot of brushes.

We have a lot of paint.

How many do you want?	How many do you have?		How many do you want?	How many do you have?	
(5 oranges)	(2 oranges)	orange	(2 sausages)	(3 sausages)	sausage
(hamburger)	(hamburger)	hamburger	(egg)	(egg)	egg
(hot dog)	(2 hot dogs)	hot dog	(candy)	(candy)	candy
(bun)	(4 buns)	bun	(chocolate bar)	(2 chocolate bars)	chocolate bar
(3 rolls)	(3 rolls)	roll	(3 cookies)	(3 cookies)	cookie
(2 sandwiches)	(2 sandwiches)	sandwich	(3 apples)	(1 apple)	apple
			(1 banana)	(5 bananas)	banana

	How much do you have?	How much do you want?		How much do you want?	How much do you have?
bowl of cereal			serving of corn		
piece of toast			serving of rice		
bowl of soup			serving of macaroni		
glass of juice			loaf of bread		
glass of milk			piece of cheese		
glass of water			ketchup		
piece of cake			cup of popcorn		
salt			mustard		
pepper					
serving of meat					

What happened?

What will you do? OR
What are you going to do?

I broke a glass.

I have to pick up the pieces.
Then I will get another glass. OR
Then I am going to get another glass.

What happened?

What will you do? OR
What are you going to do?

I lost my shoes.

I have to find them.
Then I will put them on. OR
Then I am going to put them on.

What happened?
What will you do? OR
What are you going to do?

My dog ripped up this comic book. OR
My dog ripped this comic book up.

I have to pick up the pieces. OR
I have to pick the pieces up.
Then I will buy another comic book. OR
Then I am going to buy another comic book.

What happened?

What will you do? OR
What are you going to do?

I dropped my hamburger.

I have to clean up this mess. OR
I have to clean this mess up.
Then I will buy another hamburger. OR
Then I am going to buy another hamburger.

What happened?

What will you do? OR
What are you going to do?

I spilled my milk on my jeans.

I have to wipe off my jeans. OR
I have to wipe my jeans off.
Then I will get another glass. OR
Then I am going to get another glass.

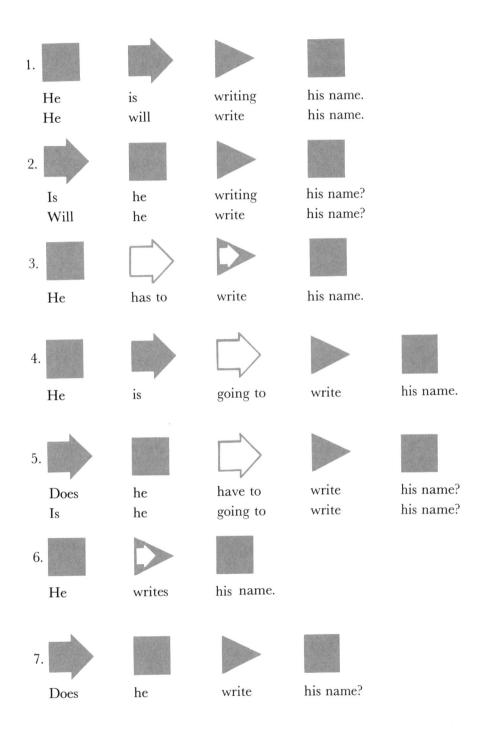

1. He is writing his name.
 He will write his name.

2. Is he writing his name?
 Will he write his name?

3. He has to write his name.

4. He is going to write his name.

5. Does he have to write his name?
 Is he going to write his name?

6. He writes his name.

7. Does he write his name?

What happened? What will you do? OR What are you going to do?

When does school start?

It started fifteen minutes ago.
You are late.

When does school start?

It will start in fifteen minutes. OR
It is going to start in fifteen minutes.
You are early.

When does school start?

It is starting right now.
You are right on time.

When does the bus leave?

BUS TERMINAL

It left ten minutes ago.
You are late.

When does the bus leave?

BUS TERMINAL

It will leave in ten minutes. OR
It is going to leave in ten minutes.
You are early.

When does the bus leave?

BUS TERMINAL

It is leaving right now.
You are right on time.

When does the movie start?

It is starting right now.
You are right on time.

FEATURE PRESENTATION

THE MONSTER IN THE SEA
1:00 p.m.
3:00 p.m.

SECRET AGENT 009
1:15 p.m.
3:15 p.m.

self test

DANGER in the YUKON
1:00 p.m.   3:00 p.m.

FRONTIER JANE
5:00 p.m.

It is 3:30 p.m.
You want to see the movie,
"The Monster in the Sea."
You are at the movie theatre.
You: When does the movie start?
Ticketseller: It started thirty
minutes ago. You are late.

1. It is 12:30 p.m.
    You want to see the movie,
    "The Monster in the Sea."
    You: ||||||||||||||||||||||||||||
    Ticketseller: ||||||||||||||||||||||||

2. It is 1:15 p.m.
    You want to see the movie,
    "Secret Agent 009."
    You: ||||||||||||||||||||||||||||||
    Ticketseller: ||||||||||||||||||||||||||

3. It is 3:10 p.m.
    You want to see the movie,
    "Danger in the Yukon."
    You: ||||||||||||||||||||||||||||||
    Ticketseller: ||||||||||||||||||||||||

4. It is 4:00 p.m.
    You want to see the movie,
    "Danger in the Yukon."
    You: ||||||||||||||||||||||||||||||
    Ticketseller: ||||||||||||||||||||||||||

5. It is 4:15 p.m.
    You want to see the movie,
    "Frontier Jane."
    You: ||||||||||||||||||||||||||||
    Ticketseller: ||||||||||||||||||||||||

6. It is 5:00 p.m.
    You want to see the movie,
    "Frontier Jane."
    You: ||||||||||||||||||||||||||||
    Ticketseller: ||||||||||||||||||||||||||

7. It is 5:15 p.m.
    You want to see the movie,
    "Frontier Jane."
    You: ||||||||||||||||||||||||||||
    Ticketseller: ||||||||||||||||||||||||||

Ask me what this is.	What is that?	It is a bar of soap.

Ask me what this is.	What is that?	It is a box of soap.

Ask me what these are.	What are those?	They are cartons of milk.

Ask me what these are.	What are those?	They are cans of soup.

Tell me what this is.

It is a glass of milk.

Tell me what this is.

It is a piece of paper.

Tell me what these are.

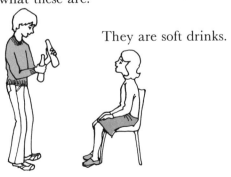

They are soft drinks.

Tell me what these are.

They are jars of coffee.

112

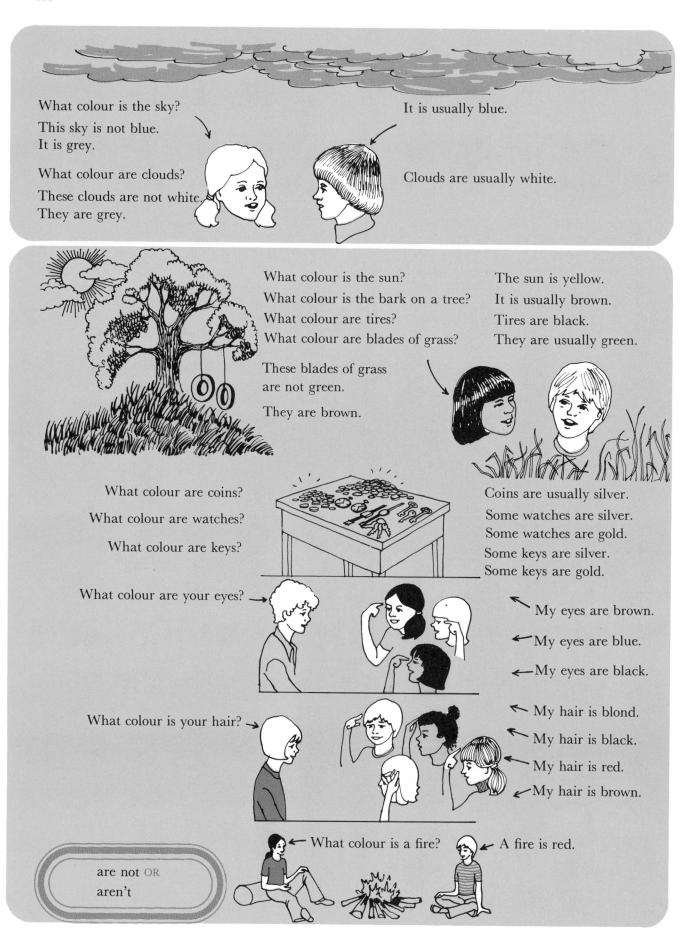

What colour is the sky?
This sky is not blue.
It is grey.

It is usually blue.

What colour are clouds?
These clouds are not white.
They are grey.

Clouds are usually white.

What colour is the sun?
What colour is the bark on a tree?
What colour are tires?
What colour are blades of grass?

The sun is yellow.
It is usually brown.
Tires are black.
They are usually green.

These blades of grass
are not green.

They are brown.

What colour are coins?
What colour are watches?
What colour are keys?

Coins are usually silver.
Some watches are silver.
Some watches are gold.
Some keys are silver.
Some keys are gold.

What colour are your eyes?

My eyes are brown.
My eyes are blue.
My eyes are black.

What colour is your hair?

My hair is blond.
My hair is black.
My hair is red.
My hair is brown.

What colour is a fire?   A fire is red.

are not OR
aren't

unit twelve

Theophilus, the thistle sifter,
While sifting a sifter full of
thistles,
Thrust three thousand thistles
Through the thickness of his
thumb.

Where are you?

I am on the teacher's desk. OR
I am on top of the teacher's desk.

I am behind the teacher's desk.

I am next to the teacher's desk.

I am under the teacher's desk.

I am in front of the teacher's desk.

We are near the teacher's desk.

We are in the doorway.
He is in a corner.

We are far from the teacher's desk.

Where are they?

They are on a plane. OR
They are on an airplane.

They are on a bus.

They are on a train.

They are in a car. OR
They are in an automobile.

They are in a truck.

They are in a boat.

They are on a horse.

They are on a bicycle.

They are on a motorcycle.

Is he on a bicycle or on a motorcycle?

He is on a motorcycle.

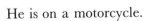

Are they on a plane or on a train?

They are on a plane.

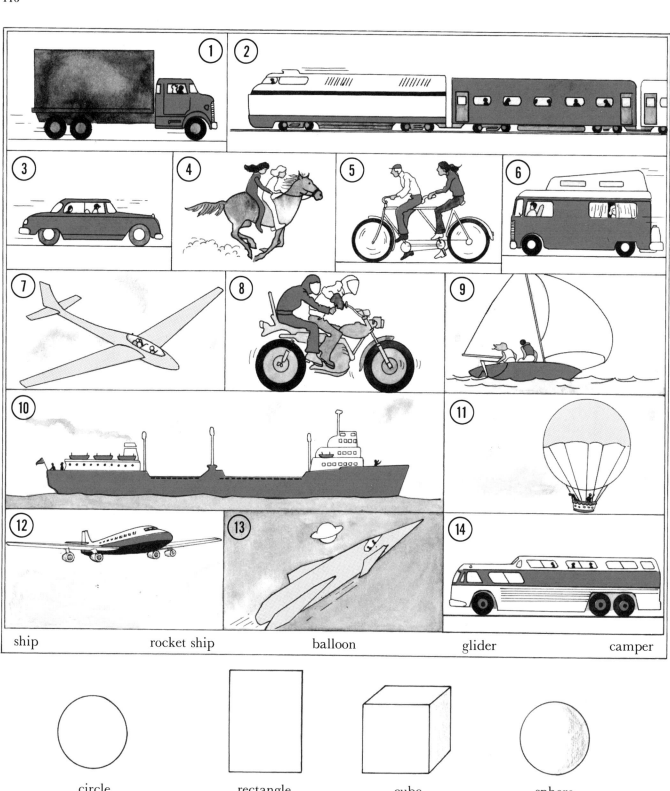

ship   rocket ship   balloon   glider   camper

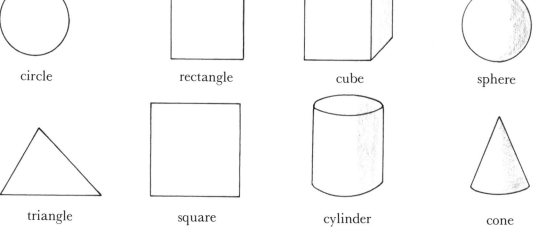

circle   rectangle   cube   sphere

triangle   square   cylinder   cone

All right.

I do not have an eraser.
Please lend me your eraser. OR
Please lend your eraser to me.

He lent me his eraser. OR
He lent his eraser to me.

All right.

I do not have any paper.
Please give me a piece.

She gave me a piece. OR
She gave a piece to me.

I cannot see your faces.
Please show me your faces.

All right.

They showed me their faces. OR
They showed their faces to me.

I have to have my eraser.
Please give me back my eraser. OR
Please give my eraser back to me.

All right.

She gave me back my eraser. OR
She gave my eraser back to me.

do not OR   cannot OR
don't   can't

Take her this boat. OR
Take this boat to her.

Help! Please bring me a boat. OR
Please bring a boat to me.

All right.

He took her the boat. OR
He took the boat to her.

I brought you a boat. OR
I brought a boat to you.

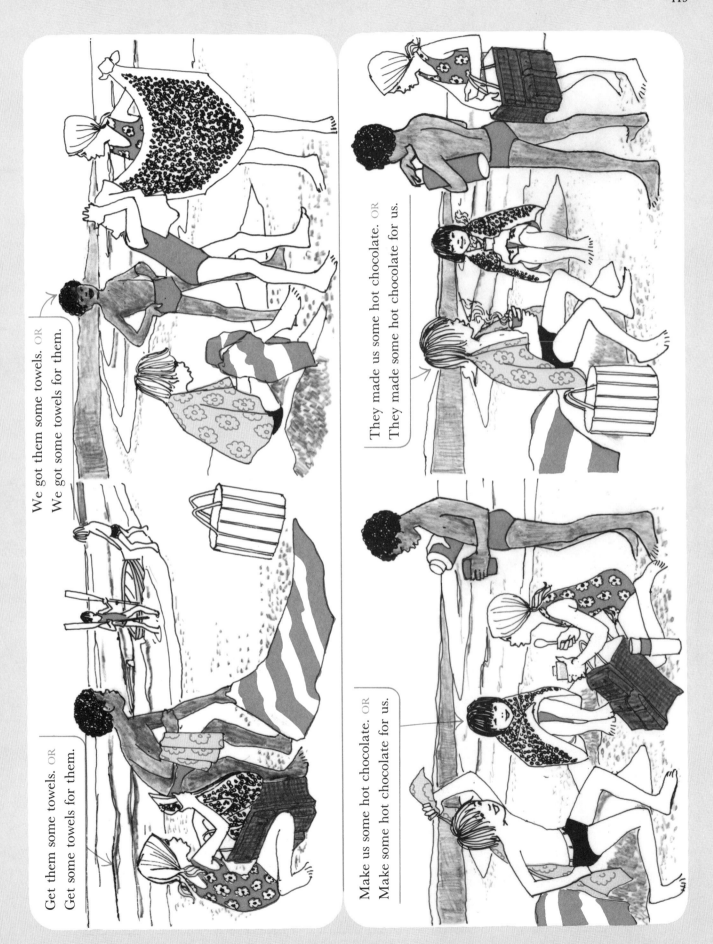

Get them some towels. OR
Get some towels for them.

We got them some towels. OR
We got some towels for them.

Make us some hot chocolate. OR
Make some hot chocolate for us.

They made us some hot chocolate. OR
They made some hot chocolate for us.

120

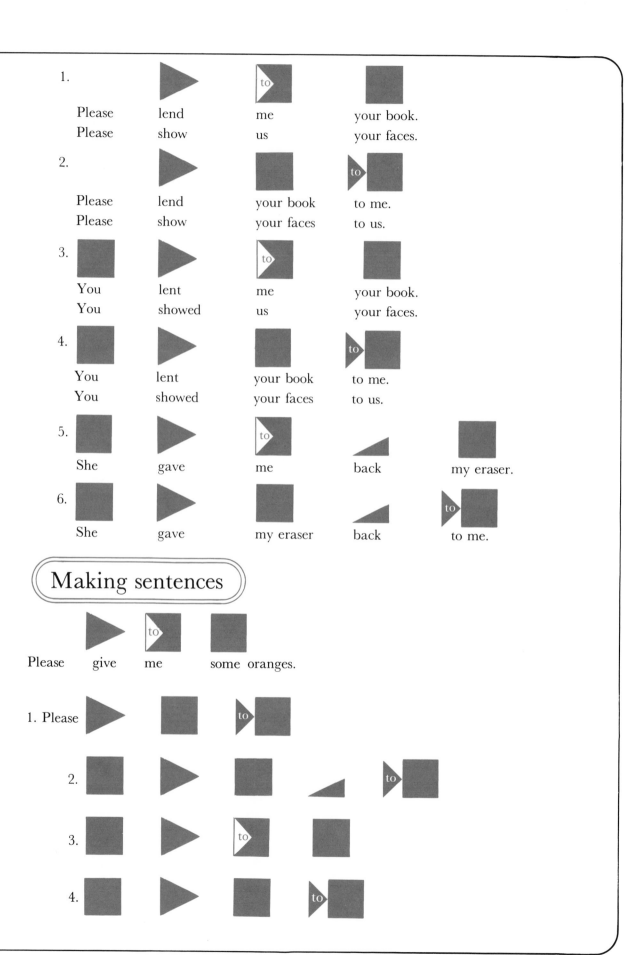

1.

| Please | lend | me | your book. |
| Please | show | us | your faces. |

2.

| Please | lend | your book | to me. |
| Please | show | your faces | to us. |

3.

| You | lent | me | your book. |
| You | showed | us | your faces. |

4.

| You | lent | your book | to me. |
| You | showed | your faces | to us. |

5.

| She | gave | me | back | my eraser. |

6.

| She | gave | my eraser | back | to me. |

Making sentences

Please give me some oranges.

1. Please

2.

3.

4.

How do they look?

He looks sad.

She looks happy.

They look angry.

He looks sick.

She looks tired.

They look hot.

She looks cold.

He looks thirsty.

They look hungry.

They look nice.

They look scared.

self test

122

124

How do they feel?

He feels sick.

They feel angry.

She feels good.

Why do you feel angry?	I feel angry because you lost my ring.
Why do you feel hungry?	I feel hungry because I did not have any breakfast.
Why do you feel good?	I feel good because I came to school by plane.
Why do you feel sad?	I feel sad because I cannot see my family.

did not OR   cannot OR
didn't   can't

VERB CHARTS

REGULAR VERBS

A

I		II		III	
clear	cleared	ask	asked	point	pointed
comb		brush		sift	
crawl		dress		start	
fill		drop		toot	
happen		help		want	
listen		jump			
open		kick			
roll		look			
seem		mix			
show		pick			
spill		pinch			
stay		punch			
		reach			
		talk			
		thank			
		toss			
		touch			
		walk			
		wash			
		watch			

B

I		II		III	
grab	grabbed	rip	ripped		
stir		stop			

C

I		II		III	
close	closed	like	liked	violate	violated
measure		wipe			
move					
please					
save					
tickle					
use					

D

carry	carried
dry	
fry	

Examples

I CLEAR the table *every day*.
I *am* CLEAR*ing* the table *now*.
I CLEAR*ed* the table *yesterday*.

IRREGULAR VERBS

1.			3.			6.		
len*d*	len*t*		hit	hit		brea*k*	bro*ke*	
ma*ke*	ma*de*		let	let		drive	drove	
			put	put		fall	fell	
2.						fly	flew	
br*ing*	br*ought*		**4.**			give	gave	
bu*y*	b*ought*		find	found		grow	grew	
ca*tch*	ca*ught*		get	got		ride	rode	
fee*l*	fel*t*		hold	held		see	saw	
hear	heard		lead	led		take	took	
leave	le*ft*		meet	met		wake	woke	
lose	lost		read	read		wear	wore	
say	said		sit	sat		write	wrote	
slee*p*	sle*pt*		stand	stood				
tea*ch*	ta*ught*					**7.**		
tel*l*	tol*d*		**5.**			come	came	
						go	went	
						run	ran	
						sing	sang	

BE

I	am	walking.			
We	are	walking.	He	is	walking.
You	are	walking.	She	is	walking.
They	are	walking.	It	is	walking.

DO

Do	I	have ears?			
Do	we	have ears?	Does	he	have ears?
Do	you	have ears?	Does	she	have ears?
Do	they	have ears?	Does	it	have ears?

HAVE

I	have	ears.			
We	have	ears.	He	has	ears.
You	have	ears.	She	has	ears.
They	have	ears.	It	has	ears.

EAT

I	eat	every day.			
We	eat	every day.	He	eats	every day.
You	eat	every day.	She	eats	every day.
They	eat	every day.	It	eats	every day.

WORD LIST